I

Spirit Lifters

ଔ James Scott Bernard ଵ

Bernard Publishing

Warrenton, Oregon 97146

ISBN 978-0-9961665-5-3

Preface

৩৮০

Over a period of twenty years I wrote spirit lifting messages. I delivered "A Thought for Today" on all of our local radio stations and published in *The Daily Astorian*.

There were positive messages designed to lift people's spirits and encourage positive action. There were special messages for Easter, Thanksgiving and Christmas. A select number of these messages are included in this small book.

My objective now, as it was then, is to offer hope and encouragement to each one of us facing the trials and triumphs as humans in a very challenging world.

Contents

 CRSO

It's a Journey

As we enter another new year, I think many of us become a little more time conscious. Along with New Year's resolutions and goals, some are looking forward to retirement—or when the kids are grown and gone. And what does the future hold?

Interestingly, in a survey of seniors now retired, seniors were asked which period of their lives were most happy and fulfilling: youth, teenage years, raising families or retirement. Almost all of the responders said the best time was when they were scrimping and struggling, raising their families.

I guess the secret to a happy and meaningful life is to recognize that all of life is a journey and to appreciate every step of the journey, and when it is filled with faith, courage, hope, lots of laughs and loads of love; a happy meaningful and fulfilling destination will be reached.

New Year, New You

CRSO

The four Rs for new life in the New Year are Reach, Risk, Rescue and Receive.

Every New Year, I try to write something to inspire myself and hopefully others.

So here's what popped into my aging head.

First, reach out and learn something new. I don't care how old we are. Learn something new. Do something new.

"We don't grow old; we get old by not growing." Gary Mack

Be not conformed to this world, but be transformed by the renewal of your mind. Romans 12:2.

Every time we learn something new, we become something new.

Second, risk looking foolish; risk sticking your neck out; risk standing up for what you believe in.

"Our doubts are traitors and cause us to lose the good we oft might win by fearing to attempt." William Shakespeare

Risk and receive the good we oft might win!

Third, rescue the unrealized potential within us. When we reach and when we risk, we rescue

"Most lead lives of quiet desperation." Henry David Thoreau

But not so, for if we reach, risk and rescue, we will receive a new lease on life for the New Year.

A Shot of Hope

❧

Each year as winter approaches most of us get our flu shots, but with days getting shorter and the nights longer there is even a greater tendency for boredom, depression and a feeling of helplessness to cause us more discomfort than the flu.

So how can we cope? By giving ourselves a shot of hope. We can create hope when things seem hopeless by sending something on ahead. We can plan trips, set new goals, help a friend, start new projects, write letters, and reaffirm our faith.

Get your flu shot, but don't forget your shot of hope.

Storms of Life

ॐ

During a recent storm, my wife and I were sitting in the dark, all bundled up, no power. My thoughts reflected my seagoing days. In a rough storm at sea, we'd heave to, putting either the bow or stern of the ship into the sea, and not fight the sea, but ride it out.

It seems to me life is kind of like that. When the storms of life batter our humble barks, don't fight them, heave to and ride it out. And remember, it came to pass.

Beating the Blues

CԳՑ

I got up the other morning thinking "Maybe there will be sunshine today." But as I got ready for my morning jaunt, I could hear the pitter-patter of rain on our roof. I thought "Oh no, not another dreary, rainy day." I guess, like most of us, I let the weather get me down.

But my next thought was, "Get over it," But how? How do you get over the winter blues when it is spring and it's still like winter?

I don't know what works for you, but what seems to work for me is a reverse of counting my blessings. I start by taking my blessings away, one by one: my family, my friends, my health, my home, my car, my freedom. What if I lost, or didn't have, any of these blessings?

Then one by one, I picture receiving them back. To top it off, I take a mental review of all the happy events in my past, and all of the positive things I have to look forward to, including, hopefully, sunshine. Give it a try.

Life, a Conveyor Belt

ᘯᘏᘯ

Life is kind of like a conveyor belt it keeps moving whether we put anything on it or not.

What exciting new plans and projects can we put on our conveyor belt of life starting right now!

For the conveyor belt of life is moving and only we can determine what is going on it.

Happiness

Webster defines happiness as having, showing or causing great pleasure.

"Most people are about as happy as they make up their minds to be." Abe Lincoln

What is happiness?

Help others get what they want and happiness happens

Always give more than you get. Have a positive balance sheet and you will never be over drawn in personal relations.

Push, plot, pilot, and pluck a path to your platform of total potential

Put yourself in the other persons place

Investigate new areas of interest

Negate all negativism

Expect the best in each and every event

Set and stick to success standards

Savor, sanctify and salvage every second

The End of the Rainbow

❦

I guess we've all thought about the "Pot of Gold" at the end of the rainbow. Reflecting on my years of living I recognize now how many times I've been at the end of the rainbow and didn't recognize it. I don't mean money (gold) but living experiences and relationships which have moved me in a positive direction. Life is a rare gift. Honor the hours, make the most of the moment and savor the second, for you may be at the end of the rainbow right now!

Brighten the Corner

CRED

Do you remember the old hymn: "Brighten the Corner Where You Are?" I guess we've all had the feeling, if only I had a better job, or lived in a different area—a place where people recognized and really appreciate me. Boy would I shine!

The secret is to "Brighten the Corner Where You Are!" And who knows where it might lead.

Getty Up Go

How do you get up and go when your get up and go has got up and gone?

You know what to do, but lack the follow through.

Just start moving; you'll soon be grooving. Better yet you'll be proving you've got what it takes to make the high stakes. How do you get up and go when your get up and go has got up and gone?

Just start moving; you'll soon be proving you've got what it takes to make the high stakes.

The Creed to Success

CREO

The creed I've found where success abounds is this ...

Happiness is within!

Happiness is now!

Happiness is appreciating and living each moment of our life.

Happiness is growing each day—finding us farther down wisdom's way.

Happiness is knowing the truth that sets us free to really become all we can be.

Speck Remover

⊂℞℘

It's so easy to look for the speck in another's eye and miss the log in our own. For it is so easy to focus on the shortcomings of a spouse, relative, neighbor or friend and miss the true goodness, small though it may be, that lies therein. This negative focus results in broken relations, divorce, and much more.

There's a tribe in Africa that has a very unique way of dealing with its members who have somehow fallen from grace. The errant tribe member is placed in the center of a circle surrounded by his fellow tribe members. One by one, each tribe member says something positive about the errant one.

Why not put a spouse, relative, friend or an acquaintance who's been a concern to you in the center of your thinking and surround them with a loving, forgiving heart, and start focusing on any and all of their positive attributes?

Grace

CREO

Gracefulness has been defined to be the outward expression of the inward harmony of the soul.

Grace, what is it?

Genial, gentle, a go giver

Wise as a serpent and gentle as a dove. Matthew 10:16

Respects the rights and dignity of others and ourselves

Allows for the imperfections of others and ourselves.

Calm, cool, caring, and composed

Embraces life, in all its varieties, with empathy, expectation and enthusiasm

Wonder of the Moment

CRSO

Wonder is an alert awareness of all that is going on about us; the fragrances, the sounds, the feel of a breeze, the kaleidoscope of color and beauty, an intense alertness to our surroundings.

As we develop a sense of wonder it makes each moment magically magnified with aliveness and meaning.

My Trail of Surprises

It's a clear, cold morning as I head out on my morning jaunt. I notice there is frost on the roofs of the houses. I enter the Warrenton waterfront trail at Seventh Place and Main Avenue.

As I turn to head north on the trail, my first surprise of the day: two huge bull elks and six elk siblings a short distance to my north. They just stand there and give me a curious stare. As I move closer, first the siblings and then the bull elk saunter off into the brush.

As I approach where Alder Creek flows into the Columbia, I hear my first woodpecker of the season pecking at a tree. A short distance further up the trail I spot a regal eagle at the top of a tree, eyeing baby buffleheads swimming below in the pond.

As I pass over the alder tide gate, I see a fishing trawler returning from the ocean with its catch, and another crab boat heading to the ocean in search of crab.

As I near the top of the trail at 13th Street, I see one of my favorite birds, the red winged blackbird, busy singing a melodious song of their own.

On my return south on the trail, I was treated to a marvelous view of the sun rising, the Astoria Bridge, the Column and Saddle Mountain. I thought to myself: This surely is God's county and my trail of surprise.

Reflection

❦

From reflection comes direction.

How much time do we spend reflecting—considering where we've been, and where we're going, our options, our paths of direction, our goals and objectives?

Are we drifters or directed persons?

From reflection comes direction.

Dream

ॐ

Have you got a dream? If not, why not? Because, like in "South Pacific," how can we have a dream come true if we don't have a dream?

A goal is a dream with a deadline. Don't kill your dream, execute it.

Beginning is Half Done

 ❦

There is a lot of truth in the old saying that beginning is half done.
We tend to live in a mañana, I'll do it tomorrow world. I'll start
eating right mañana.

The secret is to begin! That's the immediate thing. I'll do it
tomorrow is only to borrow more sorrow, only begin and you've
started to win!

Backlashed Reels

❧

I have served as a captain and guide in Alaska for the past twenty-one years. I take customers fishing for salmon, halibut and other bottom fish.

But occasionally the joy of fishing is erased by a customer hitting the wrong lever and bango, there's a big backlash on the reel, with the lines on the reel snarled and tangled in a big mess. I respond by saying, "Don't worry, it happens all the time." Then, under my breath, "How stupid can you be?" Often there will be a fish on the line, which then requires bringing the fish in, hand over hand.

Often times it seems like our lives experience a backlash. In the case of my wife and me, within a short period of time I was diagnosed with prostate cancer, followed by surgery. My wife developed a skin condition which resulted in itching, bleeding sores over much of her body, and to top ift off she had a heart attack that was remedied by a stint in her artery.

As I pondered over the situation, the analogy of a backlash reel came floating into my mind. I'm not very good at unsnarling a backlash reel so I usually put it into the hands of someone more skilled.

In our situation, we were totally at the end of our human ability to unsnarl our situation—so we have handed our situation over to the Master Fisherman.

Follow me and I will make you fishers of men. Matthew 4:19

Come unto me all ye who labor and are heavy laden and I will give you rest. Matthew 11:28

Sure, life sometimes hands us a backlash reel—but by the grace and love of God, lines can be untangled, snarls undone, free spool restored. Fishing goes on. Living goes on.

Thank you, Lord.

Patience with Me

CR&O

O' Lord thank you for your patience with me,

Help me be an extension of Thee;

Patience with others, treating them like brothers,

Feeling their pain,

Rejoicing in their gain,

Sharing their load,

Down life's bumpy road.

O' Lord thank You for Your patience with me.

Help me to be an extension of Thee.

Every Day I Do My Best

☙❧

In the Broadway Musical, The King and I, I'm encouraged to do my best for one more day, every day.

But what is our best?

Believe in yourself and your God.

Elimination negation.

Seek success in all situations.

Total commitment and utilization of your God given potential.

I'll do my best, one more day, every day.

It's Easter Time

☙❧

"Honey baked hams, bunnies and bonnets"—but what's the real message of Easter? Can it make a difference in our lives? Life can be mean and cause us to scream! We have what some have called the "chocolate bunny syndrome:" We look great on the outside—but there is emptiness within. The message of Easter is that there is a power and a presence that can fill our lives and enable us to withstand the toughest and roughest times with peace and serenity. The message of Easter is one of victory *not over* difficulties and problems, but victory *in* our difficulties and problems. We can be more than conquerors through Him who loves us, we're called to be the "light of the world, the leaven in the loaf," the crown jewel of God's creation—not down trodden failures, but valiant victors!

May the power and presence of Easter be with each of you!

Not Knowing

ॐ

Sometimes we tend to think that knowing is the key to peace of mind and happiness. But if we knew exactly what was going to happen, how things were going to be, the dynamism of life would be missing.

It is, not knowing that puts zip into life. Each day is brand new. Who knows what adventures await us?

Disappointments

I guess life throws all of us disappointments. I know I've had my share of disappointments with people, plans, projects, personal problems, you name it. But let's face it, disappointments happen but discouragement is a decision.

It is our positive response to things that are rough that builds us up—making us winning tough.

A Harvest

I got to thinking how strange it is how many of us look for a harvest in our lives when we have planted no seeds.

We look for something special to happen in our lives but have taken no action, or plans, to make it happen.

We look for letters in the mail but we have written none. We want friends, but have not been a friend. We look for a return on our money but have invested none.

Looking for a bountiful harvest in your life? Start planting seeds. Ask yourself what seeds can I start planting today?

Perfect Peace

CℛℬↃ

A ship's compass is mounted in gimbals so that no matter how heavy the seas the compass remains level. Wouldn't it be great if we had as humans some mechanism to keep our lives level when our human bark is buffeted by the rough seas of life? A strong faith offers that mechanism. It provides us with sustaining power and perfect peace.

Adventure

Force yourself into a little adventure. Learn something new. I just talked with a man who started skiing at eighty-six.

Jesus told his disciples to cast their nets on the other side.

Do something different. Put some fresh air in your life before it gets stale.

Pass It On

CRES

The other evening I was enjoying a unique dinner, shrimp with curry sauce over deviled eggs. My wife said the recipe came from a friend who had passed it on.

I thought to myself that each one of us should pass something on; be it a recipe, an idea, a way of life—but pass something on.

Let It Go

CRSO

Frustration and unrest and anxiety often result from harboring hate and resentment. It actually penalizes us more than the deed that caused the resentment.

Vengeance is mine says the Lord. Romans 12:19

Judge not that ye be not judged. Matthew 7:1

Following this advice relieves us from becoming involved in negative loss of time and life, and enables us to maintain a peaceful spirit and experience the true joy of living.

Love Never Fails

꧁꧂

Many years ago a young man was about to be released from prison. He wrote to his mother saying, "Mom I'll be coming by train through our home town in two days. I know I've caused you a lot of pain, but if you want me to come home tie a ribbon on the outer branch of the old oak tree near the tracks east of town. If not, I'll understand."

As the train approached the town the young man was so fearful that he covered his eyes to ask the man sitting next to him if there was a ribbon on the tree. As the tree came into view the man said, "Son, look." On every branch and twig of the tree, ribbons were tied.

Remember whoever you are and whatever you've done you are loved.

Purpose

CB ∞

Recognize the power of a purpose.

Have ...

A mission that matters,

A goal that gives you gumption,

A destination that defines you.

Bouncing Back

❦

On my early morning jogs, I pass by my favorite old oak tree, bent slightly from our southwesterly storms.

Each autumn, I've noticed that the last leaves to leave my favorite tree are near the top, most vulnerable to the wind. I thought to myself, "How can this be? Why sure, I've got it." It's because of the resiliency of the high branches and their ability to bounce back when buffeted by the many storms.

I got to thinking about how many of our lives get buffeted by the storms of sickness, setbacks, broken relationships, and so forth. Yet if we, like the high branches of my favorite oak tree, can maintain our resiliency, our ability to bounce back, we'll still be standing to face yet another spring.

Pin Medals on Yourself

CR80

If we are always looking for or waiting for others approval or recognition we may have a long wait and ultimately be disappointed.

The secret is to pin your own medals on. Be a success in your own eyes; give yourself credit for a job well done, an accomplishment.

Real Person

My wife surprised me by serving me real maple syrup for my waffles the other morning. I thought to myself, we all like the real thing whether it is real maple syrup, real paintings or persons. Here are three keys to being a real person.

1. Accept the fact that you are human and have limitations.
2. Always be your own unique self.
3. Call forth the tremendous God given potential within yourself and always be the real you.

Reins of Your Life

CR&O

Every time we buy into another person's anger or obtrusive behavior, it is just like saying, "Here are the reins of my life, take control of me."

Someone pulls out in front of you in traffic and you can flip a lid, honk your horn and make wild gestures, or you can say, "I refuse to put the reins of my life in someone else's hands.

Sage Advice

⊂⊃

One thing all we humans have in common is twenty-four hours each day. Be we old or young, rich or poor, we all have the same amount of time each day. How we spend that time will determine our present and our future.

So teach us to number our days that we might apply our hearts unto wisdom. Psalm 90:12

The Fog Lifted

CRSO

On a recent early morning in Alaska, as I looked out my window, I saw the bay covered with dense fog. As the morning progressed, I could see the sun slowly breaking through. Sure enough, little-by-little, the warmth and light of the sun burned off all the fog exposing a beautiful clear day.

I got to thinking how many of our lives seem to get lost in a fog of doubt, despair, uncertainty and hopelessness. Yet, if we seek and let the light of truth in and we continue to nourish with warmth our little seed of faith, the way becomes clearer. Hope returns and doubts disappear and just like a beautiful clear day, life becomes beautiful again.

The Master's Message

❧

The Master's message is not one of doctrine, dogma or creed, but rather one of simply serving others.

For when I was hungry, you fed me, naked and you clothed me, a stranger and you welcomed me, in prison and you visited me. Matthew 25:35-36

For even as you have done it unto the least of these my brethren, you have done it unto me. Matthew 25:40

The Power of Words

CRRO

Words are like arrows, once released they cannot be retrieved.

The greater the love, the larger the target, the deeper the wound.

Healing takes place, but the scar remains.

Getting on with Our Lives

☙❧

On several occasions, while drift fishing on Oregon streams, our boat would slip into an eddy out of the main stream and unless extra effort in rowing took place, the boat would remain trapped in the eddy, the circular motion of the water.

Many of our lives get trapped in an eddy of circumstances or habit that keeps us from moving on in the main stream of life. We need to take the Oars of Thought and Action, redefining our short and long term goals and move on into the main stream of our futures.

Truth

ೞ

If it is truth that sets us free. What does untruth have to do with me?

Would I choose chains instead of all that freedom gains?

O' friend, spare yourself the pain. In your life let truth and freedom reign.

What is Truth?

Tell it like it is.

Recognize reality. See things for what they really are—size up the situation.

Understanding heart. Solomon prayed for two things: wisdom and an understanding heart.

Think things through. What is going to be the result of my present action.

Have the heart to act on the truth you have.

Making the Most of the Moment

CREOR

Savor the second,

Magnify the moment,

Halo the hour,

Delight in the day.

Walk with wonder through the week

Make the most of the month, and you'll have a very good year!

Resiliency

Every time I think of resiliency it reminds me of the time I loaded the trunk of our brand new car with presto logs. It really hunkered the car down and the real surprise was when I unloaded the trunk my car remained hunkered down. It never recovered. It lacked resiliency.

Three specific areas we can apply resiliency in our lives:

1. Resiliency is being flexible enough to try something new.
2. Resiliency is being flexible enough to risk failure.
3. Resiliency is the ability to bounce back and not give up.

Love

CRSO

Love has been defined as the out living of the indwelling Christ. The scriptures tell us that love never fails.

When we practice love,

Live is an

Overwhelming

Victory

Every day

Persistence

On a trip to the Oregon coast clam digging for the first time in many years I was experiencing very poor results. I would spot the small oval crater in the sand where I was certain a clam would be. I would dig with great fury, but to no avail and no clam. My wife, digging nearby, had already dug most of her limit. What is wrong, I thought. Maybe I am not digging deep enough. Sure enough, by digging just a few inches deeper, bingo, a clam every time.

Important point, it takes almost as much effort to almost get a clam as it does to get one. It takes almost as much effort to almost succeed as it does to succeed.

Focus on the Calm

❦

How many of us either have been, or will be, diagnosed with some form of cancer? The immediate reaction is probably panic, or "Why me?" But, as I pondered this, I ask myself, "Is there any positive way to address a situation like this?" Then a thought, almost a vision, popped into my head.

One time, years ago, my wife and I left the dock in Hammond on our boat to fish for salmon in the ocean. We were later than usual on an ebb tide, and the tide was running strong. As we approached the bar, there were very high seas of eight to ten feet, very tight to each other. It looked quite frightening.

But as I looked just beyond the bar, I could see many boats fishing in calm, smooth water. It seems to me as we're faced with cancer or the other storms of life; we should keep our eyes not on the rough seas, but on the calm water that lies just beyond—perhaps a cure or a heavenly rest.

Life's Webs

CRSO

The other day I tossed a small leaf into a spider web. It made quite a tear in the web. Immediately the spider set about removing the unwanted intrusion and repairing the web. If a humble spider has the wherewithal to remove unwanted intrusions from its life, surely we, by the grace of God, should be able to removed unwanted habits, thoughts and actions from our lives.

A Positive Disposition

☙❧

It is a fact that when our disposition, our attitude, is bad even the slightest negative assault can get us down.

On the other hand, when we maintain a positive disposition, outlook, even the toughest assaults don't get us down.

The lamp of the body is the eye and if the eye [outlook] is sound the whole body will be filled with light. Matthew 6:22

Thanksgiving Time

CR&O

It's over the river and through the woods to Grandmother's house we go—turkey and dressing reflecting our blessing.

It's Thanksgiving time.

For we are told in the scriptures, to *be thankful in everything*, and *how* easy it is to be thankful when our table is full and all seems to be right in our life. But what if my health is failing, or I've lost my job or my mate, or I'm faced with financial difficulties or concern for my children?

Be thankful in everything. For when we develop the habit of being thankful for what we do have, for all that life throws at us, it transforms tragedy into triumph, bitterness into blessings, fears into cheers.

It's Thanksgiving time.

Be thankful in everything. 1 Thessalonians 5:18

Gratitude

It seems to me that gratitude is an attitude, a disposition, a posture toward all of life. Gratitude, it is counting your blessings, it gives you a spring board to a positive feeling about yourself.

It focuses upon what you have and not what you lack.

Even Jesus finding himself on a mountain side with five-thousand hungry souls said to his disciples, "What have we got to work with, five loaves and two fish." What did he do? He blessed it! He gave thanks for what he had and it multiplied. Give thanks for what you have and like magic it will multiply.

Others Perceptions

CR80

Success in human relations is recognizing that people act the way they act because that is the way they are perceiving life or a given situation.

We may not agree with or condone their behavior or actions, but recognition of this concept can give us empathy and patience to deal with even the most difficult persons.

A Strange Message

CRSO

The Prince of Peace, the central figure and the reason for our Christmas season, has a very strange message:

We're told to love our enemies,

To pray for those who misuse us,

To turn the other cheek,

To go the extra mile,

To return good for evil,

To forgive seventy times seven,

That the Greatest is servant of all.

What a strange message. But do you want to know the strangest thing? It works! It's a prescription that brings peace, from the prince of Peace.

Be Anxious in Nothing

CRŁO

We are told in the New Testament to *be anxious in nothing*, don't let anything make you anxious; anything? What about my children, my health, my finances? *Be anxious in nothing.*

Anxiety produces tension which restricts our mental and bodily functions and shortens our life.

Be anxious in nothing. Philippians 4:6

Blooming Strong

CRSO

While jogging one morning, I passed a small, old, run-down home which appeared as though it had barely survived a coastal storm. But in stark contrast to the rest of the surrounding was a small three-by-three-foot patch of beauty where the residents had planted beautiful tulips which were in full bloom.

I thought how the old home was similar to many of our lives—often battered by the trails, sorrows and disappointments in life. But yet if we keep at least a little patch of beauty, be it pleasant memories of the past, at least a mustard seed of faith or all the positive things we have left, and focus on these, our own little patch of beauty, life will remain good and we'll be given the strength to go on.

Boldness

Webster defines boldness as daring, risk taking, trailblazing.

Boldness: What is it?

Breaks down the barriers of doubt, fear and lethargy.

Open doors to opportunity.

Looks for and seeks out the possibilities in all situations.

Do it now and don't accept defeat.

Common Denominator

CR&O

When returning from Alaska, passing through Seattle International Airport, I saw a Japanese child, apparently just arriving from Japan, crying, and I was struck with the thought that regardless of our origin, we all cry and laugh in the same language.

We do all have a common denominator, a common creator.

A solution for Sorrow

ଓଃ৪ଠ

Is there any simple solution for sorrow?

Some magic potion I can borrow?

Grief has robbed my peace like a vagrant thief.

O the loneliness within, the ache in my heart, a feeling as though a part of me has died.

Has our Master lied? When His promise He cried?

Blessed are they that mourn, for they shall be comforted
Matthew 5:4

I think not!

The solution, I'm sure is to rest in Him secure, the agony will cease.

He will bring you His peace.

Courage

A real key is to acknowledge the fact that courage is not the absence of fear; it is acting, forcing ourselves to act in spite of fear. If there is no fear, no risk, no courage is required.

It seems to me that courage is the mid wife bringing birth to the otherwise stillborn potential within us.

Feelings Follow Action

How many of us have said to ourselves I don't feel like tackling that project or task right now. Or, I don't feel enthusiastic. The secret is to recognize that feeling follow actions. Just start acting enthusiastic and pretty soon, just like magic, you will feel enthusiastic. Force yourself to dig into a task and beginning is half done.

Get It Done

CR80

Leave nothing undone that you ought to do. 2 Timothy 4:5

I would venture to say that most of us are more guilty of sins of omission rather than commission, a smile to a fellow sojourner, a helping hand to someone in need, random acts of kindness, that's what living and loving is all about.

Give It Your All

CRICO

Holyfield after winning the fight from Tyson said: "When I go into the ring, I bring everything with me."

How many of us are not winning in life because we are holdouts. We are not giving life our all. Fatigue and disease comes from ease. We don't wear out, we rust out.

Whoever would save his life [not use it] will lose it, but whoever will lose [use] his life will find it. Matthew 16:25

Highest and Best Use

CRƧO

In real estate development, the true test for the property's use is: "What is the highest and best use of a particular property."

Often property suited for a much higher use is developed for lower uses. For example waterfront property is developed for parking rather than a high rise condo.

The same can be true in our lives. Are we making the highest and best use of our lives or have we settled for less than our best?

Initiative

CREO

"The world bestows its big prizes, both in money and honors, for but one thing," says Elbert Hubbard. "And that is Initiative. What is Initiative? I'll tell you: It is doing the right thing without being told."

It's Back to School

Toddlers, teenagers, and beyond are all heading back to schools and colleges to further their education and to continue their growth as persons.

How sad is it that so many of us, after completing a formal education, say to ourselves, "great, it's done," and make no further effort to grow by learning something new. Someone has said that every time we learn something new, we become someone new. Another has said we don't grow old; we get old by not growing.

It may be true that you can't teach old dogs new tricks, but the human mind is the last unexplored continent, and because of its plasticity, has an almost unlimited ability to acquire new skills and information. What we don't use, we lose.

It's no secret that at any age, the mind, like the body, needs exercise. Many of us could prevent Alzheimer's and other memory losses by keeping mentally active. Locally, we have mentally active citizens in their nineties playing bridge two and three times a week.

Why not learn to play bridge or take a community college class, but keep learning, keep growing. It beats boredom and, "Where did I put my glasses?"

It Might Have Been

"Do you know what hell would be? If I stand before God, he would tell me all the things I could have done in my life if I had only had more faith." Anonymous

"The saddest words of tongue or pen are these: It might have been." Anonymous

Just Do It

It is a truism that everything which has ever been done in the history of the world has been done by somebody; some person has exercised some power to do it.

Do you know all these things? Blessed are you if you do them. John 13:17

In life, only that which we translate into positive action counts.

Burning Issue

CRSO

As a small lad, I tried to help by building a fireplace fire for my grandmother. But the fireplace fire was sputtering, about to go out. My grandmother rearranged the pieces, added a little kindling—and bingo, a blazing inferno.

The same is true; it seems to me, in many of our lives. Things can be down to what seems to be the last little puff of smoke. Rearrange your priorities; add a little kindling of faith and initiative, and the little puff of smoke turns into a blaze of success.

You Are in Control

CRISO

The secret here is that no matter how tough a situation or circumstance may be; only you can determine the amount of significance you assign to the event.

You cannot always directly control what happens to you, but you can control the significance you assign to the event.

What Keeps Us Young

ℭℬℰ

"They say a person needs just three things to be truly happy in this world: someone to love, something to do, and something to hope for." Tom Bodett

I applaud George H.W. Bush. In spite of failing health, on his ninetieth birthday, he made another parachute jump.

I don't think we have to make a parachute jump at age ninety to keep going, to stay young. But we do need to renew ourselves daily to keep us young at any age.

Keep moving, keep going—force yourself into action, read something new, learn something new, change your routine, plan little trips, help a friend or neighbor in need.

"You don't grow old. You get old by not growing." E. Stanley Jones

Positive Reflections

CRSO

It seems as though we hear so many negatives about growing old. As I moved into my golden years, I did some reflecting on the positives. I guess my first thought was, what a blessing to have reached my golden years.

My second thought, what a great library of stored memories and experiences I have to reflect and draw upon. Thanks to my mental instant replay, I can recall past birthdays, Christmases, marriage, the births of our children, and oh so many other experiences. What a blessing.

Thirdly, my mind reflected on the fact that we can continue to grow, mentally and spiritually as long as we live. I applaud all seniors participating in the Elder Hostel programs. My own mother, at ninety-nine, even thought her eyesight was almost gone, continued to study the Bible by listening to cassette courses. My uncle, at ninety-two, still built and flew his own planes.

Finally, with all the wisdom and knowledge gained though years of living and experiences, what an opportunity we have as seniors to counsel and share this wisdom and knowledge with those who are our junior.

They say we lose what we don't use. What an opportunity for us to retain and gain by sharing our being with others.

It's Christmas Time

CRESO

Christmas wreathes and trees, carols and a cold winter breeze, it is Christmas time!

Sure we celebrate an event that took place two-thousand years ago, but what does it mean for each one of us today? It is the promise today, right now of a power and a presence that can bring us peace even in the toughest of life's times.

For the gift of Christ in you is not a figment of the imagination but a fact.

"How silently, the wondrous gift is given. Where true hearts will receive him still, the dear Lord enters in." Phillips Brooks

It's Christmas time! Let us receive God's gift which is Christ in you; the hope of glory, the promise of peace. May the peace, presence and joy of Christ be with each one of you.

Transformation

CRSO

The other night I drove by a home that, during the daylight, was very humble and plain. Wow! What happened? The humble abode had been transformed into a palace of Christmas lights. I thought how similar this is with all us humans. When the spirit of Christ— the Christ of Christmas—comes into our hearts we are transformed into radiant new beings.

Noel

It is interesting to note that Noel comes from the Latin word "Natal" or new birth. Approaching a new year, why not a noel or new birth? Try the noel formula NOEL.

New

Opportunities

Exist

Look for them

Be of Good Cheer

ॐ

What with all the chaos and turmoil in the world, and certainly at times in our personal lives as well, the following thought comes to me.

On a recent flight to Maui, just before we took off, the pilot came on the speaker and said, "Welcome aboard folks, we're expecting a fairly bumpy flight, so make certain your seat belts are securely fastened."

I guess the Captain of the Universe gave us all a similar warning as we took off in our flight in life.

In the world you shall have tribulation, but be of good cheer, I have overcome the world. John 16:33

If we believe this, we've got to believe that life is going to bring us, surely, many joys, but also many bumps in our flight. Unfortunately, we don't live in a world where everyone lives happily ever after.

With all the turmoil in the world, we can certainly agree there is tribulation. But the key word for each of us is not to surrender to fear and despair in the world, or personal problems, but to be "overcomers." And, taking it a bit further, we're encouraged, no matter what happens, to—what?—be of good cheer.

Sounds crazy, but our Master Pilot proved it on Easter. So fasten your seatbelts, be "overcomers," and be of good cheer.

Mindfulness

☙❧

Lately there has been a lot written about the subject of mindfulness. I guess it means to be alert and present to all that is going on around us.

Our creator blessed us with five senses; sight, hearing, taste, smell and touch. It seems so easy when we're not practicing mindfulness to get bored. Often our focus is ourselves and our ailments or problems. I've found out that if I get my mind off myself and become mindful of all the joy and wonder my five senses provide, my spirits are lifted.

On my Morning Trail of Surprises, I often see a regal eagle souring. I hear a woodpecker pecking on a tree, birds singing a melodious tune. I feel the touch of a gentle breeze on my cheek coming off our mighty Columbia River, the fragrance of cottonwoods blooming from way upriver. When I reach home, there's the taste of red maple syrup on my pancakes for breakfast.

Missing the blessings of your five senses? Why not treat yourself to their blessing, and activate them with a renewed mindfulness.

Always on Time

CR&O

Lord you're always on time, a time for birth and a time for death.

The sun rises and the sun sets, always on time.

The fruit of the vine, always on time.

From the warmth of the summer to the frost of the winter, always on time.

Why should we be anxious and fuss.

If we put our trust in God, who's always on time.

It's Not Too Late

༺❀༻

How many times I've said to myself, and perhaps you have too. "Boy! I wish I knew then what I know now when I was just getting started in life, what a difference it may have made. But of course we can't go back, but we can realize why it's so incumbent on those of us who have accumulated wisdom in our many years of facing the ups and downs of our lives to be mentors to the younger generation.

Retired, bored, bound up with your own problems? Find a way to get involved with the younger generation.

Volunteer, teach, share your trials and triumphs with them.

What I kept I lost what I gave I have.

How many of us go to our graves with a message in our hearts that we've never shared with family or friends that could have been a lift, a blessing to them. It's not too late. Write a letter, make a call, make a visit. As you bless, you'll surely be blessed.

A Great Day

CREM

This is going to be a great day for I am going to picture in my mind the positive outcome of a predetermined plan, and I am going to be so committed to a positive purpose that it will propel me with power and propensity to the very peak of my potential.

I was born to succeed.

I will succeed.

I am succeeding.

Today is my moment and now is my story, by the grace of God.

Epilogue

೦೩೪೦

All of the messages in this small book have resulted from personal experience. They have been a very sustaining factor, by the grace of God, in seeing me through all the toughest tests life can throw at us.

My sincere wish is that in some special way these messages may be a sustaining factor in each of your lives.

೦೩ May God Bless you! ೪೦

About the Author

❦

James Scott Bernard is a Master Mariner and Chartered Life Underwriter.

As an ordinary seaman, at age sixteen, Jim crossed the infamous Columbia River Bar. He graduated from a maritime officer's facility as a deck officer at age twenty-one and served in the Merchant Marine during the Korean War.

In college, Jim majored in business, psychology and religion. He put his education to practice as CEO of J. Bernard Insurance, Century 21 Bernard Realty, Premium Finance, and General Sales Manager of a Ford Dealership.

Along with his wife his wife Cherie, Jim operated a fishing charter business out of Hammond, Oregon at the mouth of the Columbia River.

Jim served twenty-one years as a captain and guide at Yes Bay, Alaska taking guests fishing for salmon, halibut and other bottom fish.

Cherie and Jim live in Warrenton, Oregon, less than a mile from the Mighty Columbia River. They are proud parents of four children, fourteen grandchildren, and twenty-one great-grandchildren. They have been happily married for sixty-seven years and have always been blessed by a living and loving Lord. Jim is an elder in the Presbyterian Church.

Jim is the author of six books. In addition, his articles appear in *Barron's, Dealer World, The Daily Astorian,* and various national sales journals.

Note: A Chartered Life Underwriter holds the world's most respected designation of insurance expertise. The CLU designation is awarded by the American College of Underwriters after completion of four year's study in business marketing, rate making, finance, and so forth. Many insurance company executives hold this designation. When Jim received the designation in 1962, only thirty others in Oregon held the designation.

Books by James Scott Bernard

Alaska Fishing Adventures (2015)

Inspirational Nautical Poems and Prose (2015)

Making the Principles of Success a Habit (2016)

Positive Poems and Rhymes (2015)

Positive Thoughts for a Profitable Day (2015)

Spirit Lifters (2016)

The Adventures of a Young Merchant Sailor (2015)

Contact

For comment or additional information, Jim Bernard can be reached at:

JamesBernard711@aol.com

503-680-2366

James Scott Bernard

Author/Publisher

870 NW Fir Avenue

Warrenton, Oregon 97146

USA

Made in the USA
Middletown, DE
20 August 2022

71687834R00056